Smithso

All About Dogs

Maggie Fischer

PRE-LEVEL 1: ASPIRING READERS

 LEVEL 1: EARLY READERS

- Basic factual texts with familiar themes and content
- Concepts in text are reinforced by photos
- Includes glossary to reinforce reading comprehension
- Phonic regularity
- Simple sentence structure and repeated sentence patterns
- Easy vocabulary familiar to kindergarteners and first graders

 LEVEL 2: DEVELOPING READERS

 LEVEL 3: ENGAGED READERS

 LEVEL 4: FLUENT READERS

Silver Dolphin Books
An imprint of Printers Row Publishing Group
A division of Readerlink Distribution Services, LLC
9717 Pacific Heights Blvd, San Diego, CA 92121
www.silverdolphinbooks.com

Printers Row Publishing Group is a division of Readerlink Distribution Services, LLC.
Silver Dolphin Books is a registered trademark of Readerlink Distribution Services, LLC.
The Smithsonian name and logo are registered trademarks of the Smithsonian.

All notations of errors or omissions should be addressed to Silver Dolphin Books, Editorial Department, at the above address.

Reviewed by Darrin Lunde, Collection Manager, Department of Vertebrate Zoology, National Museum of Natural History, Smithsonian.

ISBN: 978-1-68412-441-1
Manufactured, printed, and assembled in Rawang, Malaysia.
First printing, February 2021. THP/02/21
25 24 23 22 21 1 2 3 4 5

For Smithsonian Enterprises:
Kealy Gordon, Product Development Manager
Jill Corcoran, Director, Licensed Publishing
Brigid Ferraro, Vice President, Consumer and Education Products
Carol LeBlanc, President

Image Credits: Superstock, Inc., Thinkstock

Every effort has been made to contact copyright holders in this book. If you are the copyright holder of any uncredited image herein, please contact us at Silver Dolphin Books, 9717 Pacific Heights Blvd, San Diego, CA 92121.

Man's Best Friend

Dogs are **loyal** pets.
Dogs are called "man's best friend."

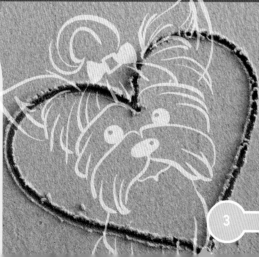

Paw-some Puppies

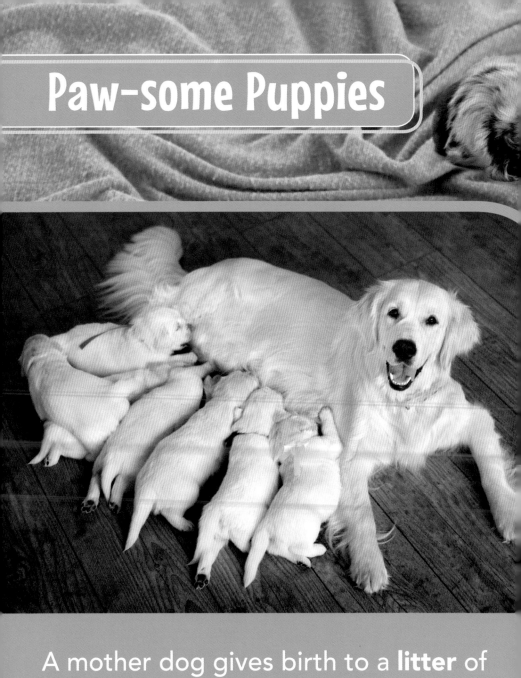

A mother dog gives birth to a **litter** of many babies at once.

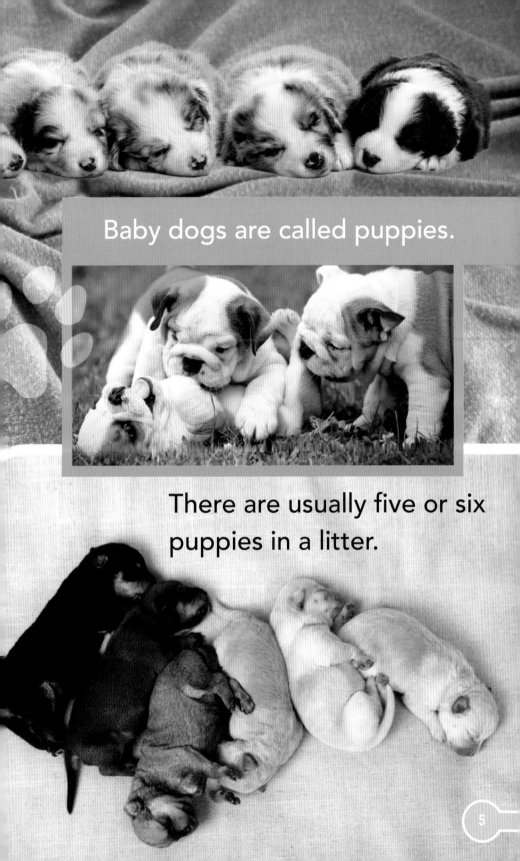

Baby dogs are called puppies.

There are usually five or six puppies in a litter.

Paw-some Puppies

Puppies can't open their eyes until ten days after birth.

Puppies sleep a lot.

Puppies are very social, and love to play.

Curly Coats and Fluffy Tails

Dogs come in different shapes, sizes, and colors.

Their size, shape, and color depends on their **breed**.

There are over three hundred breeds of dogs.

Curly Coats and Fluffy Tails

The fur that covers a dog's body is called a **coat**.

Dogs have different types of coats.

Some dogs have curly coats.

Some dogs have long coats.

Some dogs even have spotted coats.

Curly Coats and Fluffy Tails

Dogs can have ears that point up or ears that hang down.

Dogs can have long, fluffy tails or short, fuzzy tails.

Some dogs have just a short stub for a tail.

Bow-Wow Behavior

Dogs wag their tails when they are happy.

Dogs cannot sweat.

When dogs get hot, they start **panting**.

Panting is heavy breathing that helps
dogs cool down.

Puppy Chow

Dogs are **omnivores**.

They eat vegetables, grains, and meat.

Some human food is bad for dogs.

Dogs cannot eat chocolate, almonds, or garlic.

These foods are poisonous to dogs.

Tricks and Training

Dogs can be taught tricks like sitting, staying, and fetching.

Some dogs compete in competitions and win trophies.

Dogs can win prizes for running fast, jumping far, and being **obedient**.

Strong Senses

Dogs have a very powerful sense of smel

A dog's sense of smell is over ten thousand times better than a human's.

Dogs can hear very well too.

Dogs on the Job

Dogs are very good at following instructions.

Dogs make great workers!

Some dogs help police officers by sniffing out missing people.

Police dogs wear a vest so people know they are working dogs.

Dogs on the Job

Seeing-eye dogs help people who are blind.

They help guide their human.

But don't distract a guide dog by petting it when it's on the job!

GUIDE DOG

Dogs on the Job

Sled dogs can pull sleds in snowy places.

Sled dogs are also used in racing competitions.

Huskies make great sled dogs because they love the snow!

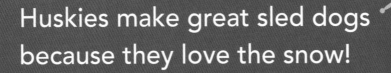

Perfect Pets

Dogs make great pets and great workers!

Dogs are loyal, friendly, and smart.

Dogs are definitely "man's best friend."

All About Dogs QUIZ

1. What are baby dogs called?
   a) Kittens
   b) Doggies
   c) Puppies

2. What kind of dog is often used as a sled dog?
   a) Golden Retriever
   b) Husky
   c) Chihuahua

3. What is an omnivore?
   a) An animal that eats vegetables, grains, and meat
   b) An animal that swims
   c) A working dog

4. Which of these foods is bad for dogs?
   a) Chocolate
   b) Ham
   c) Carrots

5. How many different breeds of dogs are there?
   a) Ten
   b) Over three hundred
   c) Fifty

6. When they are happy, what do dogs do?
   a) Lie down
   b) Bark
   c) Wag their tails

Answers: 1) c 2) b 3) a 4) a 5) b 6) c

GLOSSARY

Breed: a sub-group of animals with similar traits

Coat: layer of fur that covers a dog's body

Litter: animals born together

Loyal: faithful

Obedient: willing to follow instructions

Omnivores: animals that eat plants and meat

Panting: breathing heavily